Keep Me Safe at Home and in My Community

A handbook on Safety for Young Children and their Families

By
Rebecca Adler

Illustrated by
Susan Anderson

AuthorHouse™
1663 Liberty Drive, Suite 200
Bloomington, IN 47403
www.authorhouse.com
Phone: 1-800-839-8640

First published by AuthorHouse 4/29/2009

ISBN: 978-1-4389-0585-3 (sc)

Printed in the United States of America
Bloomington, Indiana

This book is printed on acid-free paper.

authorHOUSE®

When I am at a pool, I must stay with an adult and listen at all times.

I will wear sunscreen, so that my skin will not get burned and hurt me.

I need to learn to swim and
understand the rules of the pool.

I will never push anyone near the water, so that no one will get hurt.

Swimming Pool Safety

Playground Safety

I will not put my hands on the windows especially if they are open. That way I will not get hurt.

Car Safety

I will learn about street signs and what they mean.

Street Safety

If anybody touches me in my private places, I will tell my mommy or daddy right away.

Strangers

I must never play with matches or candles. Fire starts and spreads easily. I can blow out my birthday candles with an adult watching me. My family can practice fire safety at home with me.

My family needs to have smoke alarms throughout the house. An adult needs to check the batteries and change them twice a year.

I will not jump on my bed, or on other furniture.

Bathtubs can be dangerous. I must be watched by an adult.

I need to keep my hands clean, especially before I eat, and after I go to the potty.